THE
COWBOY
TRADE

THE
COWBOY
TRADE

WRITTEN AND
ILLUSTRATED BY

GLEN ROUNDS

HOLIDAY HOUSE
NEW YORK

CONTENTS

THE
COWBOY
TRADE

COMING

WILD WEST
SHOW
LONDON · PARIS · ROME

THE COWBOY
IN TV,
FILMS AND FICTION

For more than a hundred years traveling Wild West shows and Western films have drawn enthusiastic crowds in all parts of the world, and playing cowboy is a popular pastime of young boys everywhere.

Even now countless millions of folk, both young and old, squat nightly in front of their television sets, breathlessly following the latest adventures of their favorite Western heroes.

The colorful characters they watch, however, seem to come in only two styles—Good Guys, wearing

huge white hats, and Bad Guys who wear equally
large black hats. Both kinds are almost invariably
shown wearing at least two huge revolvers in holsters
hanging from wide, sagging cartridge belts, and these
holsters are almost always tied to the wearer's legs by
long untidy leather thongs.

Occasionally these screen cowboys do bring a herd
of scruffy-looking cattle up the trail from Texas, or a
posse of White Hats pursues an equal number of
Black Hats at breakneck speed along the skyline,
through the Badlands or across the Rio Grande. Now
and again a fearless U.S. marshal and his gray horse
are seen camped for the night in some dry gully, wait-

ing only for daylight before resuming their relentless pursuit of a killer, a bank robber or evildoer of similar stripe.

But otherwise almost all of the screen and television cowboys' time would seem to be spent in Dodge City and other such resorts. They are shown riding their horses into saloons and dance halls, harassing tenderfeet or simply gathering on the sidewalk to see the stage come in from Abilene, Kansas City or some other far-off place. When not engaged in these simple activities they regularly stage good-natured but deadly gun fights that leave the streets of the TV towns littered with the corpses of the losers.

A television watcher might well wonder what useful work these fellows did, and how they earned the money they spent so recklessly in the saloons and dance halls of the towns. For that matter one might well ask why men who spent so much of their time indoors, or idling on boardwalks shaded by wide porches, had need of such large hats that were obviously designed to protect their owners from the scorching sun of the treeless plains.

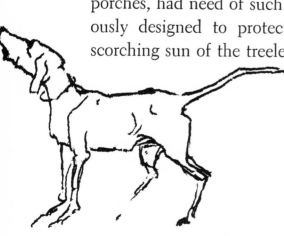

It is, of course, an historical fact that in the days of the Old West cowboys had a well-deserved reputation for sometimes being more than a little wild when they came to town. And it is also a fact that there were certain quarrelsome individuals who made a practice of shooting sometimes fatal holes in the persons of folk unfortunate enough to have offended them in some small way.

But by and large these exciting episodes were surprisingly few and far between. In real life the cowboy worked at a monotonous and demanding trade that had little resemblance to the film and TV version. He

spent his daylight hours—and often much of the night as well—in the saddle. He dealt with violent and uncooperative horses and cowbrutes in a land that offered little in the way of comfort or entertainment. Often as not he slept for weeks at a time on the ground, in fair weather or foul. His food was either seasoned by grasshoppers and dust in dry weather, or made soggy by rain in wet.

All in all, one thing taken with another, it was anything but an easy life, and the average cowboy stood a greater chance of being killed or crippled by lightning bolts, falling horses or tangled ropes than by a gunman's bullets.

THE BEGINNINGS OF THE COWBOY BUSINESS

The cowboy trade really had its beginning when the early Spanish settlers brought their tough long-horned cattle into what is now northern Mexico. Here, on their huge New World ranches, they found that men and animals were cheaper than fencing, so they let their growing herds run loose instead of keeping them in pastures as they'd done at home.

Grass was good and water plentiful in that brushy country, and the Spanish cattle quickly adapted themselves to the new conditions. Tough, aggressive, fast on their feet and armed with long, needle-sharp horns, they had little to fear from the wolves, mountain lions and other predators that infested the country. So the herds prospered and multiplied rapidly.

At the same time, living under these free conditions, they soon became as wild as the deer and other game animals whose territory they shared. So as time went on the Mexican ranchers began to find it more and more difficult to lay hands on their property at branding or butchering time.

Cattle confined in pastures could be driven into a convenient fence corner and caught by means of a rope noose fastened to a long pole. But here there were no fences, and the cattle themselves were more like wild game than domesticated stock.

At the first sight of a horseman these creatures scattered, running as fleetly as deer, and holed up deep inside the almost impenetrable thickets that blan-

keted much of that country. And even when they had somehow been flushed out into the open it was still almost impossible to round them up into any sort of compact herd that could be driven from one place to another. Instead, each animal picked a direction that suited his purpose, and set out to quit the country as rapidly as possible. Often enough, all a crew of vaqueros—the Mexican cowboys—had to show for a long day's work were exhausted horses and a mounting sense of frustration. So from necessity these men began to invent equipment and work out new ways for dealing with this wild new breed of cattle.

They braided long slim ropes, or reatas, of rawhide strips well greased with tallow, and learned the trick of casting a running noose accurately around the neck of a dodging steer while riding at top speed through brushy thickets or across gullied, broken ground. And

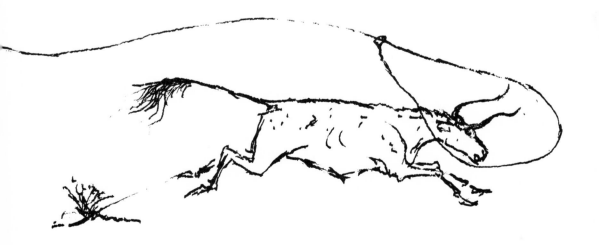

they built short stout snubbing posts, or saddle horns, into the pommels of their saddles so that their horse's weight could be used to throw or hold the uncooperative animal on the other end of the rope. And over the years they became skillful in the use of horse and rope, as well as knowledgeable in the ways of the wild longhorns.

Even so, a great number of calves escaped the attention of the branding crews each spring, and as the herds increased and spread in all directions from their original ranges, the number of these unbranded mavericks multiplied also.

By the time our Civil War ended and discharged soldiers from both armies began to drift to Texas in search of land, work or adventure, they found the country heavily stocked with the wild longhorns. The ones without brands legally became the property of anyone who could catch and mark them. Money and

jobs were scarce in that country, so certain of the more adventurous traded for Mexican saddles and reatas and set out to learn the cattle-catching trade.

At first it was a sort of hunter's business, the animals they caught being sold to ranchers or driven in small herds to nearby settlements or army posts to be butchered. But it wasn't long before a few more enterprising men began to buy up cattle and hire crews to drive them in herds of two thousand or more up the plains to railheads in Missouri and Kansas. From there they were shipped to meat packers in the East.

It was a risky business with Indians, outlaws, flooded rivers and stampedes a constant threat. Losses on the way could wipe out a man's entire investment, but the chance of profit also was great and for a few years the number of herds sent up the various trails rapidly increased.

In the beginning all cattle brought into Missouri and Kansas from Texas found ready buyers waiting. But more and more came up the trail each summer until at last they were arriving faster than the railroads could haul them away, and many unsold herds had to be wintered on the plains.

These cattle did well on the prairie grass in spite of the cold northern winters, so it wasn't long before men began to consider the possibility of raising their own beef on the open range instead of depending on the long drives from Texas.

The riders who brought the first herds up from Texas had been mostly cattle-catchers, or drovers— men who could move large herds from one place to another without undue loss. When they had delivered one herd they rode back to Texas and brought up another. But only a comparatively small number of men were engaged in this business.

However, as the ranches spread northward up the unfenced plains from Oklahoma through eastern Colorado, Wyoming and into Montana, the cattle became valuable property, rather than a variety of wild game, and crews of horsemen were needed to prevent their loss by theft or straying. And that was the real beginning of the cowboy business of Wild West fame.

These first cowboys were mostly Texans, ex-soldiers and other drifting adventurers. But soon word of the adventurous lives led by these men began to catch the imagination of farmers, factory workers and storekeepers of the East, and writers for newspapers, magazines and dime novels found a ready market for Western stories—the more lurid the better. Farm boys and boys from the cities reading these exciting tales found their own lives dull by comparison and went West by the hundreds to learn the cowboy trade.

THE COWBOY'S DAY
STARTED EARLY

In real life the cowboy's working day usually began well before daylight. A favorite range story tells of a drifting rider, who had bedded down in a strange bunkhouse well after midnight, being wakened at four o'clock and remarking to no one in particular, "A man can sure spend the night quick in this country!"

After groaning his way into his hat, pants and boots by the light of a smoky coal oil lamp or lantern, a man pulled the tarpaulin up over his bed, took his turn at the bunkhouse wash basin then trudged off to breakfast at the ranch house. By first daylight everybody had finished eating and drifted down to the corrals to meet the wrangler bringing the remuda in from the night pasture. Without waiting for a factory whistle to blow, each man shook out his rope and moved into the corral to snare his mount for the day.

When everybody had saddled up, the rancher or his foreman assigned the jobs to be done and the parts

of the range to be ridden. Then one by one the cowboys rode off in their various directions.

Riding alone with no one to talk to but himself or his horse, a man spent the day attending to the unexciting but necessary chores he was paid to do. Few cowboys, except in the very early days of the business, ever had occasion to engage in shoot outs with rustlers, fight hostile Indians, or even ride with a sheriff's posse.

Instead, in summer there were dozens of widely scattered springs and water holes to be looked into and, if necessary, cleaned out. Anyone who has done it will tell you that wading about in the mud and muck of a trampled water hole, trying to clear it out with a rusty, broken-handled shovel is not likely to sweeten a cowboy's temper. Nor does it improve the appearance of his boots any to speak of, and those fellows generally set a lot of store by their footgear.

Where other water was scarce, windmills were used on many ranges to pump water from wells. A casual passer-by in dry country might well be pleased by the sight of the big fan spinning high overhead and the sound of the rusty pump rods clanking as they brought up the little stream of clear water splashing into the troughs for the thirsty cattle. But few realized that the contraptions had gears and cogwheels and that every so often some grumbling, sweating cowboy had to carry tools and a bucket of grease up the rickety ladder to the tiny platform at the top of the tower to grease and adjust the machinery. It wasn't the sort of job men fought for.

In unfenced country cattle grazed pretty much as they liked in scattered bunches of twenty-five to one hundred, so the riders were always on the lookout for any that were straying too far off their home range. Such stragglers, when found, had to be gathered up and driven a few miles to where better grass or water would encourage them to stay closer to their own territory.

At certain times of year cattle developed lumps and sores caused by the larvae of the warble fly hatching from eggs deposited beneath their skins. Or the fresh scabs on newly branded animals would be attacked by magpies, who often tore great raw patches out of the unfortunate victim's hides. These animals, when discovered, had to be roped, thrown, and their sores painted with a sticky, foul-smelling salve the cowboy carried on his saddle—a necessary job, but not one to bring a man much pleasure.

After the spring thaws, when cattle were thin and weak from the long winter, they often got themselves mired down when they ventured onto boggy flats in search of the first green grass. The cowboy finding

such a creature had to get a rope around its neck and drag it onto firm ground with his horse. And that also was an unglamorous temper-fraying chore for all concerned. The cow was seldom grateful, nor upset by the fact that in saving her life the cowboy had made a muddy mess of his clothes and prize throw rope.

The climate itself brought little joy to a man working out in the open day after day. Hot dry winds that stirred up choking clouds of fine alkali dust often alternated with sudden violent thunderstorms. But whatever the weather the cowboy continued riding, uphill and downhill, across dry sage brush flats and into or around deep washouts, checking the whereabouts and welfare of the cowbrutes wearing his employer's brand.

On rare occasions the monotony of his day might be broken by some exciting episode such as meeting a rider from another range, or even the sight of a rattle snake. The stranger gave him a chance to exchange news or range gossip, and the snake provided one of the few excuses to draw and fire his six-shooter. But mostly a cowboy simply rode from morning until night, doing range chores and hoping he'd get back to the ranch before suppertime.

Then, after playing a few hands of seven-up or reading a Western story magazine, if there was one in the bunkhouse, a cowboy went to bed so as to be up early and ready to do much the same thing the next day.

TOOLS OF THE
COWBOY'S TRADE

Cowboys were horsemen by trade, and they liked to think of themselves as men who could ride anything with legs on the four corners and hair on the outside.

The truth is, however, that real-life cowboys, like men in other trades, varied greatly in their skill, and even a top hand might have difficulty staying aboard a really energetic bucking horse. Almost every outfit had certain men who seemed to enjoy matching wits and strength with ill-tempered and uncooperative outlaw horses, but such activities were not usually en-

couraged by either the ranchers or their foremen
when they interfered with the work at hand.

The cowboy's job was to look after the welfare of
of wild range-bred cattle. Each day he rode long miles
over rough lonely country, and his chores usually kept
him about as busy as he wanted to be without having
matters complicated by the antics of an unreliable
horse. His mount was transportation and, if properly
trained, one of the tools of his trade. Even the best of
such horses was seldom the sort to be safely ridden
by ladies or small children, and every cowboy knew
that, given a chance, almost any horse would try to
throw him. A good workman tried to make sure that
this happened as seldom as possible, and left the rid-

ing of outlaws to men who specialized in such violent action.

Every cowboy, as a general thing, owned one or more saddle horses that he used when going about his personal affairs or traveling through the country in search of work. However, the condition and quality of his personal mount might vary from month to month, depending on his luck at cards, judgment of race horses or his ability as a horse trader. But on the job his mounts were furnished by the ranch he worked for.

Depending on the size of the spread, a ranch might keep up a remuda consisting of fifty to a hundred and fifty saddle horses. The quality of the saddle stock provided for the riders varied from ranch to ranch, and even the horses in any one remuda varied widely in quality and temper. All were considered broken to ride, but the extent of their reliability and cooperation was not guaranteed.

When a cowboy rode into a ranch and was hired, he turned his own horse loose in the corrals, found a place to hang his saddle and threw his bedroll and war sack on an empty bunk in the bunkhouse. Later, when the horse herd was brought in he would be assigned his string. Sitting beside the new man on the corral fence, the rancher or his foreman would point out one horse and then another in the milling herd until the necessary number had been made up. On a small spread each man might have four or five horses in his string while on a larger one, or at round-up time, he might be assigned ten or twelve.

There was a sound reason for this. In busy times, such as roundups, horses were ridden hard and a cowboy might change mounts several times a day. The saddle horses, except in dead of winter, were fed neither hay nor grain, but were simply put out to graze at night and on their days off, and even in normal times such a grass-fed horse was unlikely to stay in

good condition if he was ridden every day without rest.

Once he had had his horses pointed out to him and heard their names if they had any, a cowboy was expected to be able to pick his mounts out of the remuda at any time of day or night. For as long as he stayed on with this ranch these horses belonged to him as surely as if he held a bill of sale for them. And to tamper with a horse from another man's string without his express permission could lead to quick and violent trouble.

It was only natural that the men already on the job would have had the pick of the best horses, so that the late comer's string, taken from the culls, might well turn out to be something less than a complete joy to him. He could complain, and often did, but usually with little result. So for the first week or two on a new job he spent much of his time learning the habits, gaits and peculiarities of his mounts while hoping for the best.

A cowboy at work didn't ride continually at a gallop in moving picture fashion. Instead, he usually kept his horse at a swinging walk or a little jarring jog. Alternating between these two gaits, he could ride long distances without exhausting his mount. For his own comfort a man picked the horse with the easiest gait for long rides. Another might have a bone-breaking trot but be knowledgeable and helpful as a roping horse.

Still another, with little else to recommend him, might have the barrel build and disregard for water that makes a good swimming horse—handy for bringing a man across flooded rivers without getting his boots full of water.

A man quickly catalogued the worst of the bad habits among his mounts. It was well to know which one insisted on indulging in a little sudden violence in the mornings before settling down to work so as not to be taken by surprise. To be thrown right after

breakfast, before even leaving the corrals, could sour a man's outlook for the rest of the day.

Another thing it was important for a man to know was whether or not any of his mounts would stand "ground tied." Even in a country where trees, fences and hitching posts were few and far between a cowboy occasionally had to dismount to do some chore or other at a distance from his horse. In such cases most horses would stand as securely as if hitched, as long as the reins were dropped over their heads. There were certain individuals, however, who didn't profit from such training and only waited until the rider was busy elsewhere before heading back for the ranch alone. So it was well for a man to know ahead of time which of his horses were trustworthy in this respect. Riding boots were never made for long walks across country.

After his horse the cowboy's most important piece of equipment was his saddle. Not only did he spend most of his waking hours in it, day after day, but its make and condition were taken by strangers as a

badge of a man's standing in the cowboy trade. A beginner might ride a hull of dubious quality or of obscure origin, but unless he was entirely without ambition—or intending to return soon to farming or sheep herding—he immediately set about saving his money for something better.

Saddle catalogues in the bunkhouses were always as tattered and well-thumbed as the Western story magazines. Names of saddle-makers were well known, and cowboys argued as hotly over the comparative merits of famous Fort Worth, Denver, Cheyenne and Miles City products as folk do now over makes of automobiles.

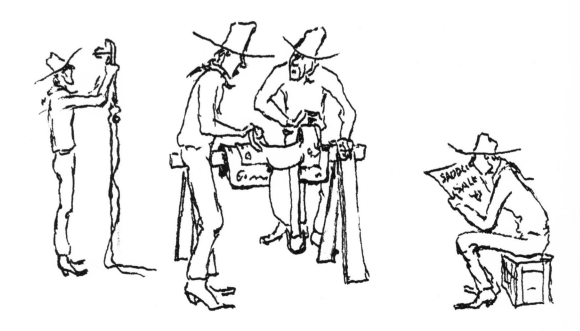

Cowboys in town could spend hours in the local saddlery looking at the new models, even when they had neither money nor any intention of buying.

Most bought their saddles ready-made, but as expensive as they could afford. However, almost every cowboy's ambition was to someday have one made to his own specifications, with his brand or initials hand-tooled on cantle and skirts.

Styles varied considerably from range to range. Texans used large saddles with wide skirts, which gave their horses some protection from the thorny thickets where much of their work was done. Those who could afford it favored much silver, and elaborate stamping and hand-tooled decoration on their equipment. Towards the northern ranges both dress and horse gear grew progressively more somber, and north of Oklahoma a man with a silver-mounted saddle or other fancy trappings was looked on with some suspicion until he'd proved he was something more than just a fancy dresser.

But no matter what its make or condition, a cowboy's saddle was the last thing he parted with when he fell onto hard times. He might risk his bench-made boots, his fancy spurs, his silk shirt, or even his best Stetson on the outcome of a horse race or some similar sporting event. But he parted from his saddle only as a last resort, or when he was foolish enough to believe he was betting on a sure thing.

A man going by train or stage to another far-off range, or Back East to spend the winter with his sister, might sell off or give away all his equipment except his saddle. That he took with him, neatly sewed into a grain sack to prevent its being rubbed or scarred on the way.

To say of a man that he'd sold his saddle meant that he was quitting the business.

Another tool of the cowboy's trade was his rope. He might speak of it as his twine, whale line, catch rope, throw rope, lasso, lariat or maguey. In Mexico the rope was usually a braided well-greased rawhide, sometimes as long as forty or fifty feet, while on the plains a shorter rope of hard twist Manila was the usual thing. Whatever the material or the length, the standing part of the rope ran through a small eye, or honda, set in the end to form a free-running noose. In use, a loop of the proper size was shaken out and held in the right hand, while the rest of the coil was held loosely in the left. A cowboy afoot, catching a horse in the corral, didn't swing his rope overhead. Instead he dragged the noose at arm's length behind him. Then, when ready to make his cast, he swung with a side-arm motion, outward and up. When the loop was directly over the proper horse's head, a twitch on the rope running freely through the roper's hand dropped it in place and jerked it snug.

Almost anyone, with practice, could learn to use a rope reasonably well this way, and a cowboy who couldn't rope his own horse was not particularly well thought of on the range. To do the same thing from the back of a running horse following the violent turnings and twistings of an animal trying its best to leave the country was another matter.

At such times it took considerable skill and close attention to be able to keep one's seat while trying to shake out a loop and get it swinging around one's head ready for the cast without tangling it among one's horse's legs. In this sort of work the help of a well-educated horse was important, for as soon as the noose settled home around the running critter's neck or legs things got really violent. The rider would quickly take a turn or two of his end of rope around the saddle horn while the horse braced himself for

the shock of the roped animal hitting the other end. If everything went well, the cow or steer would be thrown with enough of a jar to keep him comparatively quiet for a minute or two. Then while the trained horse backed up as necessary to keep the rope tight enough to prevent the animal from getting up, the cowboy dismounted and did whatever was to be done.

These were everyday roping skills that most working cowboys had, but some men were experts able to throw a noose in any number of complicated ways. To catch a running animal by both front or both hind feet was a useful skill in certain situations.

So to have a rope in good condition, one that would uncoil smoothly without kinks, was important to a cowboy. In an emergency he might use it to picket his horse if he had to camp far from home. And on occasion men have been known to use their good ropes to impress horse thieves and other evildoers with the disadvantages of a lawless life. But as a general thing he was very careful with it, and it was not only bad manners but downright unhealthy to use another man's rope without his permission.

SMALL POSSESSIONS AND EQUIPMENT

There were many cowboys with steady jobs, men who worked summer and winter year after year for one ranch. But the greater number were migrant workers, appearing when extra hands were needed at roundup or branding time, or to help trail beef herds to the railroad, and drifting on when the job was finished.

Such a man seldom accumulated much in the way of personal plunder beyond his horse, saddle and bedroll. Even an old timer with a permanent home in some bunkhouse could usually store his lifetime's gathering in an old apple box under his bunk.

A large percentage of the men who took the first trail herds of long-horned Texas cattle up the plains to the railheads in Missouri and Kansas after the Civil War were discharged soldiers, and they wore whatever they could lay their hands on. Coats and pants bought second hand from civilians, or parts of old uniforms—blue or gray. Black cavalry hats rode alongside city-style derbys, and footwear ranged from dragoon boots to cowhide brogans. All in all these fellows were a nondescript looking lot, and in spite of the fact that they really started the cowboy business they would have difficulty convincing today's Western motion picture or TV producers that they were genuine cowboys.

But as the cattle business established itself on the plains, with ranches scattered from Texas to Canada, the cowboys' dress and equipment became more specialized and distinctive.

Hats varied considerably in size from one part of the country to another, with the widest brims and the highest crowns being found in Texas. From there northward the brims became progressively narrower and the crowns lower, so it was possible to make a good guess as to a stranger's home range simply by looking at his hat. But whatever the size or style, the man who could afford it usually bought an expensive and durable Stetson, for his hat was more than simply a part of his costume.

Besides being a head-covering, the hat had a hundred other uses the maker probably never thought of. The wide brim protected a man's eyes from the glare of the sun in dry weather and shed water when it rained, so that chilling streams of rain drops didn't run down his neck. The hat could be used in an emergency to blindfold a bad horse while he was being saddled or to slap and encourage one that was trying to buck.

That same hat could be used to fan a slow-starting fire or to carry water to put it out when time came to break camp. Waved in the air it was a signal that could be seen a great distance, and slapped across the face of a bad tempered cow it could discourage her from trying to interfere with the necessary things being done to her calf by the branding fire. So it is small wonder that no matter how old and battered it became it was a cherished possession of a man whose possessions were few. It was the last thing he took off at night and the first thing he put on in the morning. And woe betide the man ill advised enough to take liberties with another's hat!

Even in winter a cowboy almost never wore a cap. In very cold weather he might tie his scarf over the

crown of his hat and under his chin to hold the brim against his ears to protect them from the freezing wind. The scarf had other uses, also. Much of the cowboy's work was done in thick clouds of choking dust stirred up by the moving herds or by the constantly blowing wind. At such times, the scarf was worn as a mask over the nose, serving as a sort of respirator.

Boots were another item of dress that a cowboy set great store by. These were not the short-barreled, wide-topped cactus-catching creations one sees today. Instead, the old-timers liked them tall and close fitting, coming nearly to the knee. They usually had loops or long leather hound's-ear grips on the tops to help with the difficult problem of getting them on. Cowboys were vain of their small feet and usually wore their boots as small and tight as possible, but there was a practical reason for this, also. The narrow build and pointed toe made it easy to find the stirrup when mounting in a hurry, and just as easy to free one's feet in the event of being thrown or having one's horse fall. The high peg heels also had a practical use:

a man working on the ground in the roping corral could dig those heels into the dirt and brace himself against the struggle of the uncooperative calf or horse on the other end of his rope.

Everyday boots were usually made of plain leather, although most had considerable decorative stitching, often in several colors of thread. But for dress a man could really let himself go. Cutouts in the tops might be backed up by leather in several contrasting colors and combined with elaborate machine stitching to make eye-filling patterns of butterflies, birds or monograms. And only the uncaring or the improvident wore ready-made footgear, for it was a matter of pride for a man to have his boots hand-made over his own special cast.

Spurs were worn both for use and for decoration and, as with almost all other items of cowboy gear, styles differed from one part of the country to an-

other. Men in Texas and the Southwest mostly favored large rowels, long gooseneck shanks and, sometimes, heavy silver decoration. Some even had tiny bells fastened to them, and thin jingly chains under the insteps so that a man carried something of a musical commotion with him, either riding or walking.

Farther north on the plains, where fancy outfits were looked on with considerable disfavor, spurs were smaller, made of plain iron, and had a small sharp rowel. These worked efficiently enough when a man had occasion to bring some shortcoming to his horse's attention but brought little joy to the wearer.

However, even on those more soberly dressed ranges it was not unheard of for a cowboy to have a pair of the fancy Texas-style contraptions hidden away in the bottom of his war sack for wear on special occasions like trips to town. With the straps properly adjusted, and by swinging his feet a certain way, a

cowboy could make those huge rowels spin and ring against the boards of the sidewalk at every step. This took a little practice but the resulting jingle and the admiration of the townfolk were worth all the trouble it took.

Chaparajos were first worn by the Mexican vaqueros, the "brush poppers" who spent a great share of their time riding deep into the almost impenetrable chaparral and mesquite thickets to bring out their wild long-horned cattle. They were a sort of legging, made of heavy bull hide attached to a leather belt, with a wide bat–wing flap that covered part of the horse's sides as well as the rider's legs, protecting both man and animal from the sharp thorns and branches.

The Texans, who learned much of the cowboy trade from the vaqueros, shortened the name to "chaps," and wore them as they took cattle northward up the plains. Later the northern cowboys, who had little need for protection from brush and thorns, changed the style of the chaps as they had much of the other Texas equipment. They did away with the wide bat–wing and ended up with what amounted to a pair of seatless leather breeches, worn over their regular clothes to protect their legs from cold wind and rain. Some had a line of leather fringe down the outside seam, and maybe half a dozen nickel-plated conchas securing the lacing thongs. But as a rule they were more utilitarian than decorative. Every range had stories of the Eastern bride or visiting female relative who set out to sew a new seat in what they thought to be a pair of someone's scandalously worn out leather pants.

For dress-up occasions certain fashion plate types, even on the northern ranges, kept fancy bat—wing chaps, often with cutout designs backed by colored leather insets and pounds of brass rivets worked into

monograms and the like. And for a while the craze for angora chaps, made of goatskins with the long hair still on, invaded the plains from Oregon and Washington. At first these were either black or white, but later on some of the more style-conscious had them dyed bright orange. However, enthusiasm for the fad soon dwindled. In wet weather the goat fur had a right rank smell and horses used to more conservative leather trappings often took violent objection to both the looks and the smell of the things. Also, they tended to give a man afoot a slightly ridiculous appearance—something like walking about with his legs in two furry nail kegs.

Almost without exception the cowboys in films and on TV go armed at all times, indoors and out. All wear at least one heavy revolver, and a surprising number wear two.

It is, of course, a fact that in the old days certain quarrelsome fellows with reputations for being professional bad men did occasionally wear two guns at one time. But this was unusual. Even by wearing one pistol slung low, with his holster tied to his leg, a man advertised the fact that he considered himself a gun-fighting specialist rather than a working cowboy. Such fellows had few friends and generally practiced their trade by shooting holes in one another—for pay, whenever possible.

Sometimes these gunfights occurred as the Westerns show them, the shooting done face to face after the proper warning. But in real life the so-called Code of the West was not too carefully observed, and often enough a badman's career was ended by his being "dry gulched"—shot from ambush by another of his kind.

Almost every cowboy did own a gun, of course, and in the early days of the business when Indians, thieves

and outlaws of various kinds were fairly common, it was as much a part of his dress as his hat. But instead of being worn low on his leg, television-fashion, it was usually belted high and snug around his waist. This way the gun was less likely to get in the way of the cowboy's hands or rope, or to be jarred out of the holster as he worked at his trade.

In real life there were some cowboys who were reasonably good shots with a six-shooter, but the deadly fast draw types who could shoot the buttons off a dude's shirt were few and far between. To become such a fancy gunman took hours of practice, day after day, and the average cowboy worked at other chores —matters that took up his time from sunup to dark.

When he did have time to himself, he usually found something more entertaining to do than practice fast draws and fancy shooting. Besides, cartridges were expensive, and the cowboy's pay was small.

The average cowboy, as a matter of fact, was a reasonably peaceful fellow, and only a small percentage ever had occasion or inclination to engage in gunfights.

Even so, a six-shooter was useful in many ways. It could be used as a hammer (it was a good idea to first remove the cartridges from the cylinder, however) for driving staples when it was necessary to make temporary repairs on a barbed wire fence. It could be used to put a crippled horse or cowbrute out of its misery or to kill snakes. In an emergency a rider could sometimes turn a stampeding herd by firing past the leaders' heads, and three spaced out shots was a universal distress signal.

A cowboy having his picture taken for the folks Back East either drew his six-shooter and held it at the ready across his chest or wore it with the holster pushed prominently to the front. This made it plain to all and sundry that no matter how young and un-impressive he'd been at home, out here he was a man to be reckoned with.

Camping miles from the ranch and finding himself without knife or can opener, an enterprising fellow could open a can of peaches or tomatoes with a couple of well placed shots. Opening a can of sardines this way, however, was seldom successful. And, happening to visit a neighboring ranch and finding nobody home, a man without a pencil could write a note with a lead bullet, providing he first could find a piece of paper and providing, also, that he knew how to write.

So, all in all, even the most peaceful cowboy found his six-shooter a handy tool of many uses.

Beyond these few tools of his trade, the average cowboy's possessions didn't amount to much. He usually carried a yellow slicker rolled up and tied behind the cantle of his saddle and maybe a cloth or

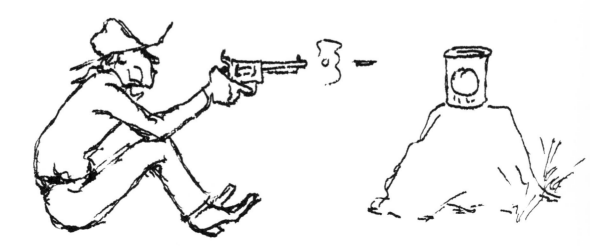

sheepskin coat if the weather was cold. His bedroll was a few blankets or tattered quilts in a strip of canvas fourteen to sixteen feet long and six feet wide. Sleeping out, the excess canvas could be folded under his bedding to make a windproof sleeping bag, and in case of rain the extra length made a small tent over his head. All other small bits of personal plunder—his razor, extra shirt, socks, scarf, old letters, saddle catalogues and other such treasures—went into his war bag. This was a cotton sugar- or grain-sack, and was carried rolled into his bedding when he traveled.

COWBOYS AFOOT

Cowboys, as a general thing, liked to think of themselves as horsemen, men who lived and worked almost exclusively in the saddle, and Western films and literature have spread this impression far and wide.

It is a well–known fact that viewing the world from the back of a horse gives even the scrawniest man a new outlook and feeling of importance. And cowboy boots with their high heels and pointed toes were never made for comfortable walking, so it is not surprising that for any journey of more than a few yards a cowboy rode, if possible.

But nonetheless, there were a surprising number of jobs on any ranch that could not be done from horse-back by even the most ingenious cowboy.

After the roundup was finished and strays from other ranges had been started for home, these summer chores began. There was still a certain amount of riding to be done, checking water holes, grass and drifting cattle. But there were also corrals to repair and pasture fences to build.

Dismounted cowboys might be sent jolting off on all-day trips with teams and wagons to cut posts and poles in the cedar breaks or along the river bottoms. As they swung their axes and strained to load heavy timbers, they grumbled and complained mightily. It was not only the humiliation of the farmerish work they minded, but the sight of their boots becoming muddy and scratched and scuffed brought them much unhappiness. However, a job was a job, and a man did it or quit.

Sometimes a crew would spend weeks digging post holes in the hard sunbaked ground, blistering their hands on the unfamiliar shovel handles. Then they'd tear their clothes and fray their tempers rolling out and stretching miles of barbed wire.

Water for both cattle and horses was always a problem on the range, and many ranchers built earth dams to catch run off water from rain or melting snow. Such a job meant more days of hot dusty work on foot following horse-drawn plows and scrapers or using picks and shovels.

Then in the fall when the grass began to ripen, there was wild hay to put up. A large ranch might keep a hay crew busy for a month mowing, raking and stacking winter feed. After a spell of such chores a man could become right homesick for his saddle.

And between these jobs, there were still others that had to be done on foot. The blacksmith's shop was an

important part of the ranch equipment, and much time was spent there shoeing horses and repairing wagons. Occasionally a cowboy might even find himself sent to repair a henhouse or pigpen! It was a far cry from the picture of the carefree horseman riding across the plains at a high lope, firing his pistol at all and sundry, or rescuing Eastern ladies from runaway stagecoaches.

So it was small wonder that after a few weeks of these dull chores the cowboys began to look forward to Fall Roundup—even with its hard work and long hours in the saddle. For the same reason, Western story magazines of all kinds were popular in the bunkhouses. The cowboys on paper led vastly more exciting lives than the readers, and such disagreeable subjects as barbed wire stretching and pigpen repairing were seldom mentioned.

ROUNDUP TIME

Ranch owners whose cattle ran loose over several hundred square miles of unfenced country faced a considerable problem in keeping track of their property. In spite of the fact that men rode more or less regularly over the range to turn back stragglers, cattle still drifted away by ones and twos, and sometimes in larger bunches. They might be driven by storms, the search for better grass or simply by a desire to travel. But for whatever reason, animals wearing the brands of neighboring ranches could usually be found on anybody's home range.

So twice a year, in late spring or early summer and usually again in late fall, the ranchers sent their round-up crews out to sweep the ranges and sort things out. The calves were born in early spring, and being valuable property, it was important that a man get his brand on the spring crop before some enterprising but unscrupulous neighbor got there first with his own rope and branding iron. So spring was calf-branding time. The fall roundup caught some unbranded calves missed in the spring, but its main purpose was to gather the animals to be shipped to market and to move the rest of the herds onto winter range.

Organizing a roundup took much thought and planning, for the entire range had to be thoroughly combed and all cattle brought to central locations with as little confusion and wasted motion as possible. Camping places had to be decided on ahead of time, making sure there was sufficient grass, water and space to hold the herds as they were collected.

Extra riders were hired and additional saddle horses thrown into the remuda. The roundup cook spent his time making lists of supplies to be brought from town and scouring pots, skillets and dutch ovens while he got his chuck wagon ready to go.

On starting day everybody was up and moving long before daylight. As soon as they'd eaten, the riders threw their bedrolls on the wagon, caught their horses and rode out to take their assigned places in the dragnet that would sweep the first day's area.

Later, the cook climbed onto the high seat of the chuck wagon, gathered his lines and drove out, followed by the wrangler and the remuda. In an hour or two they reached the first camp ground. While the wrangler unhitched the teams and dragged up a supply of firewood, the cook got out his pans and kettles and started his cook fire.

During the forenoon the first small bunches of cattle were brought in and spread out to graze on the nearby flats. As more and more were combed out of the thickets and gulleys by the converging circle of

riders, the herd on the flats continued to grow until the entire sweep was finished. Then guards were set to make sure the results of the morning's hard riding didn't suddenly decide to go back to where they'd come from, and the rest of the crew rode to the chuck wagon. Picking up cups, tin plates and hardware from the tub by the wagon, they filed past the fire to have their plates filled with beef, biscuits, potatoes and whatever else the cook had seen fit to stir up. The better a roundup cook was at his trade, the shorter his temper seemed to become, so the cowboys were careful not to arouse his wrath by stirring up unnecessary dust or by complaining about the quality of the food. As each man finished, he scraped his plate and threw it and his other eating tools into the wash tub, then went to where the wrangler was already holding the remuda in a rope corral and caught a fresh horse for the afternoon's work.

A little way off from where the herd was being held, the branding crew had already built their fire and had

the branding irons heating. The foreman would have sharpened his pencil and gotten his tally book ready, and if it was a big roundup with the possibility of large numbers of cattle from other ranches being mixed in the herd, those owners would have sent men (reps) with tally books to keep a record of all calves branded here for their employers.

When everything was ready, the scattered herd was crowded into more compact shape, and the first ropers rode quietly into it while the guards kept the cattle from scattering. This work called for a skillful roper and a knowledgeable horse, for the calves had to be roped and dragged to the fire without stirring up the wild cattle any more than necessary. Almost as soon as the roper had picked out a calf and identified the brand on its mother, a good horse would be moving smoothly among the closely packed animals to put the man in position for his cast. And as soon as the noose was in place and twitched tight, he turned without command to drag the bawling, struggling creature to the branding fire.

The roper called out the mother's brand and an entry was made in the proper tally book, with a note as to its sex—whether bull calf or heifer. One of the branding crew reached over the calf's back, grasped flank and foreleg, and threw it heavily on its side. With one man sitting on the calf's head and another keeping its hind legs stretched out, the noose was loosened and taken off. Then, while the rider rode back to the herd, recoiling his rope and shaking out a new loop, the proper iron was brought from the fire and the brand seared into the calf's hide. After being branded, each calf had one or both of its ears notched with a distinctive earmark that would identify it even when its brand couldn't be seen. None of this took much time, and when the creature was let up it usually left that place as rapidly as possible. If its mother had followed it out of the herd, both were driven off some distance to be held separate from the herd be-

ing worked. Otherwise it went alone, protesting and bawling for its mother.

This was hot, sweaty, dusty business of a kind seldom shown on TV. As the work went on the clouds of dust rose higher and higher, and men had to shout to be heard over the clamor of calves blatting for their mothers and cows bawling for lost calves. Occasionally an old cow, objecting to the rude treatment her calf was getting, would provide some excitement by trying to tree the men around the branding fire. But mostly it was the sort of hard, monotonous work that made men wonder why they'd ever decided to be cowboys. And there was no extra pay for overtime.

When the last calf had been dragged to the fire, and the foreman and the reps had pocketed their pencils and tally books, the herd was turned loose to water and graze while the tired men and horses drifted back to the chuck wagon.

Horses were unsaddled and turned into the remuda, and the men who would take turns guarding

the herd after it finished grazing caught up their night horses and staked them on grass nearby. After supper bedrolls were taken from the wagon and spread on the ground. There was some idle talk. Then the first of the night guard rode out to where the cattle were bedding down, and the rest crawled into their blankets. The kind of work they'd been doing didn't encourage them to sit up late around the fire singing songs or playing games. At five o'clock the cook would be banging on his triangle, starting them on another day like the one just ended.

This work went on day after day, until the last calf had been branded and tallied. Except in special circumstances the chuck wagon and the remuda moved each day to a new place, and each morning the riders went out to sweep in all the cattle on another part of the range. Afternoons they sweated and roped and branded. And day and night they listened to the bawling of the cows and calves. They were scratched by thorns and branches as they chased uncooperative animals out of wild plum and choke-cherry thickets and risked their necks riding down the steep sides of cutbanks and washouts. There was always the chance of being crushed under a falling horse or being drowned crossing a flooded river.

Sleeping on the ground week after week was no great pleasure even in dry weather and in rainy times was a thing no one would do by choice. And the food, even at its best, left something to be desired, although no man in his right mind would say so in the cook's hearing. So, what with one thing and another, a new man at the business couldn't be blamed for deciding it was a hard, dull trade quite different from what the Western story magazines had led him to expect. A great many sold their saddles and went on to other things after one such job.

THE COWBOY
IN WINTER

Ranch work went on the year round. After the fall roundup was over, the beef herds were driven to the railroad, the hay crews finished their work and the extra riders were laid off. The ones kept on the payroll then settled down to six months or so of cold, hard disagreeable work.

During the great blizzards that regularly swept the plains, herds might turn their tails to the bitter wind and blinding snow and drift miles from their home range. When the weather cleared, cowboys bundled into heavy sheepskin coats and with scarves tied over their ears rode out to find and bring them back. Other herds trapped in low places by drifts of deep soft snow had to be driven or dragged to safer ground.

Holes had to be chopped through the ice at the watering places so the stock could drink. In particularly bad times, weakened cattle had to be urged and hauled to their feet every morning and loads of hay from the stacks scattered on the feeding places.

None of these were particularly attractive ways to spend a winter, so it is not surprising that many cowboys left the range and moved into town during the cold months. Some, who'd saved their wages, rented themselves rooms, ate ready-made meals at the cafés and spent their time playing cards, trading horses or simply resting up from their summer's work. Others, less provident, looked for jobs. They were seldom

particular about the kind of work as long as it was inside and close to a hot stove. Some worked as hostlers around the livery stables, others as bartenders and swampers in the saloons, and some even clerked in stores—anything to be in out of the snow and wind.

Still others, not liking the confinement of inside jobs but unable to find work on any of the ranches, drove stage, or freighted feed, or baled hay and other supplies from the railroad to inland towns and ranches. That also was cold, monotonous work, but being carriers of news and mail in a country where newspapers were scarce, and those few that came arrived weeks late, they were welcomed everywhere. So, all in all, it was a comparatively sociable life, considered by many to be well worth the disadvantages.

Another fairly popular way to spend the winter was what was called riding the grub line. A cowboy who wasn't particularly interested in working either inside or out, or who simply wanted to see the country without expense, had only to tie his bedroll behind his saddle and start riding.

All sorts of people, ranchers, freighters, horse-traders, hunters or cowboys looking for work, were constantly on the move from one place to another, and on the plains where the towns and road houses were far apart, it was important that a traveler be able to find food and shelter for his overnight stops. So it was the custom of the country that any stranger overtaken by night was free to ride into the nearest ranch and be invited to put up his horse, throw his bedroll on a vacant bunk in the bunkhouse and put his feet under the table at mealtime.

A rancher's wife could never be sure how many mouths she'd have to feed at any meal. But these strangers, like the freighters, carried news and gossip, so they were able to make a fair return for hospitality.

As with any such custom, however, there was a fairly strict code of manners involved in its smooth operation. Nobody was turned away no matter how crowded the place or how poor the people. Nonetheless, the stranger was expected to ask permission to

put up for the night. And in the morning when he was ready to leave, he asked what he owed for himself and his horse. When he'd been given the ritual answer of "Glad to have you," he was free to leave. However, if a man had money he might, if he liked, slip a silver dollar into the paw of a child without giving offense. And it is a fact that ranchers' children usually made it a point to be out in plain sight when such possibly generous strangers were leaving.

Most of these visitors stayed only overnight, unless caught by a blizzard or some other complication. But a grub-line rider, interested only in spending the winter as easily and inexpensively as possible, might stay on for days or even a week or more before moving on to the next ranch.

Of course he was expected to help out with chores and maybe would be set to cutting a supply of firewood. But even so, a man who really set his mind to it could live right well and see a considerable scope of country just riding the grub line.

THE COWBOY
IN TOWN

At best it was a hard, demanding life the cowboy led. His hours were long and entertainment was scarce. So, when he did make one of his infrequent trips to town, after weeks of riding alone or listening to the constant bawling of cattle from the dusty drag of a slow-moving trail herd, it was not really surprising that he sometimes became overenthusiastic in his enjoyment of the pleasures of civilization.

On occasion certain showoff types did ride their horses into saloons and even into dance halls. Others took great pleasure in riding through the streets at top speed, firing their pistols into the air (or in some instances, at any lighted window that happened to catch their attention) and practicing shrill cowboy yells. Generally they meant no real harm, simply being full of high spirits like boys yelling, running and fighting when first let out of school.

However, there was another reason for much of the wild behavior—it was expected of them. From the very beginning of the cowboy business the people in the East were fascinated by the tales of the wild, violent lives led by these colorful horsemen.

It wasn't long before writers were traveling West in droves to see these strange fellows and to write

their stories down. They quickly discovered that the more wild details they added to already improbable tales the better their Eastern readers liked them. The cowboys, too, read and enjoyed these Western stories, which were so much more exciting than their own lives. So it is not surprising that when they came to town some of the more impressionable fellows tried a little too hard to live up to the reputation the Eastern newspapers, magazines and dime novels had given them.

Even so, the colorful violence was usually perpetrated by a comparatively small but lively minority. The average cowboy was content to spend his short stay in town in a dogged and determined effort to get

as much of what he considered high living as possible before his time and money ran out.

In those days a cowboy seldom owned more than one or two changes of clothes, and arrangements for bathing and laundry out on the range were skimpy to say the least. After a few weeks or months on the trail, both the man and his clothes tended to be a little over ripe for the noses of townsfolk, some of whom were said to bathe as often as once or twice a month.

So the average cowboy's first stop, after putting his horse up at the livery stable, was usually the general store, where he bought a change of clothes from the skin out before heading for a bath at the barber's shop.

After a session in the back room, soaking and scrubbing himself in the big tub with buckets of hot water, he finally put on his clean clothes and was ready for a shave, haircut and whatever additional services the barber might have to offer. These things were an almost unbelievable luxury after the months of hard, dirty living.

When he had finally been scrubbed, trimmed, massaged and anointed and stepped out onto the street, the cowboy sweetened the air for yards around with a combination of the smells of talcum powder, hair tonic, bay rum and goodness knows what else. At last he was ready to take advantage of whatever civilized refinements the town had to offer. The sa-

loons, gambling joints and dance halls usually did a roaring business, and on occasion there was a certain amount of deadly gunplay.

But not all cowboys had either the money or inclination for such expensive and vigorous entertainments. These others spent much of their time buying ready-made meals in the town's eating houses or window shopping for clothes, boots, saddles and other fancy gear. Horse trading was a popular pastime with some, while others were content to spend their time simply walking up and down the streets admiring the strange sights. Even the more violent ones—men who found a childish pleasure in the sound of breaking windows or bar mirrors after months of listening to nothing but wind, creaking saddle leather and the bawling of cattle—usually came around later to pay for the damage they had done.

But it made little difference what sort of entertainment the cowboys chose; the result was always the same. In a surprisingly short time the diligent townsfolk separated them from their money and sent them on their way back to the far-off ranges with their pockets empty. However, being simple fellows, the few days in town would have furnished them with material for endless tales to be told and retold during the long weeks ahead.

THINGS ARE
DIFFERENT TODAY

The cowboy business still goes on, but many things
have changed since the days of the Old Wild West.
A few of the larger ranches still run their cattle on
ranges covering hundreds of square miles and even
operate old–fashioned roundups complete with chuck
wagons.

But more and more, as the value of beef animals
has increased, they are raised in huge pastures behind
fences that keep them from straying. Cowboys are
still needed to see to the welfare of the herds and to

move them from place to place. There are still calves to be branded, sick or injured animals to be doctored and windmills to be greased. But often as not the cowboy now drives a jeep or pickup truck from pasture to pasture, hauling his horse, ready saddled, in a trailer hooked behind.

Nowadays the bunkhouse often holds a television set, and like everybody else the cowboys are great watchers of the Westerns. So it is small wonder that the style of their town-going clothes is greatly influenced by the outlandish getups worn by the heroes of the Western serials or the more popular of the Country Music fellows.

Once you could pretty nearly pinpoint a man's home range after one look at his clothes and gear, but now the fellow in the skin-tight embroidered jacket, thirty-gallon hat and double-breasted, pearl-buttoned shirt might well be either a cowboy dressed for town or a supermarket bag boy on his way to his night job playing guitar over the local TV station.

But in spite of all the changes the cowboy business is still a tough, demanding trade. And there are still plenty of the genuine brass bound, copper riveted, bronc' stompin' cowboys around if only you look in the right places.